SPORTING CHAMPIONSHIPS
WIMBLEDON

Jeff Kubik

WEIGL PUBLISHERS INC.

Published by Weigl Publishers Inc.
350 5th Avenue, Suite 3304, PMB 6G
New York, NY 10118-0069

Website: www.weigl.com

Library of Congress Cataloging-in-Publication Data

 Kubik, Jeff.
 Wimbledon / Jeff Kubik.
    p. cm. -- (Sporting championships)
 Includes index.
 ISBN 978-1-59036-697-4 (hard cover : alk. paper) -- ISBN 978-1-59036-698-1 (soft cover : alk. paper)
 1. Wimbledon Championships--History--Juvenile literature. 2. Tennis--History--Juvenile literature. I.
Title.
 GV999.K83 2008
 796.34209421'2--dc22
 [B]

                                2007012107

Printed in the United States of America
1 2 3 4 5 6 7 8 9 0 11 10 09 08 07

Project Coordinator
James Duplacey

Design
Terry Paulhus

CONTENTS

What is Wimbledon?

Lawn tennis is an outdoor racquet sport. It is played between two players or between two teams of two players. Wimbledon, or "The Championships," is the largest and oldest lawn tennis championship in the world. Wimbledon is named for the area of London where it is held. The **All England Lawn Tennis Club (AELTC)** and the Lawn Tennis Association (LTA) run the **tournament**.

Wimbledon has been held since 1877. It takes place over a two-week period in June and July. Players from more than 60 countries come to Wimbledon each year. Winning the Championships is an honor every player hopes to achieve. Attendance at the event has grown each year from a few hundred to nearly 500,000.

There are five main events in the championships. They are Gentlemen's **Singles**, Ladies' Singles, Gentlemen's **Doubles**, Ladies' Doubles, and Mixed Doubles. Wimbledon also features Junior and invitational events. Junior events are for players who are 18 years of age or younger.

The Ladies' Singles Trophy is a copy of a 17th-century pewter plate made by German artist Caspar Enderlein. Venus Williams won the trophy in 2000, 2001, and 2005.

Invitational events are for players who are invited to take part in the tournament by the AELTC. Events include 35 & Over Gentlemen's and Ladies' Doubles and Gentlemen's Wheelchair Doubles.

Wimbledon is one of the four major national or **Grand Slam** tournaments. The others are the French Open, the United States Open, and the Australian Open. A player who wins all four of these tournaments in a single year is said to have won the Grand Slam of tennis.

CHANGES THROUGHOUT THE YEARS	
PAST	**PRESENT**
Tennis balls were white, hand-sewn, and made of leather and cloth.	Tennis balls are yellow, with a hollow rubber core and a nylon cloth covering.
Racquets were made of wood.	Racquets are made of lightweight metals.
Ladies wore long dresses, corsets, and boots.	Ladies wear tennis skirts and tennis shoes.
About 200 fans attended the first Wimbledon.	More than 500,000 fans attend the event.

The Wimbledon Trophies

The Gentleman's Singles Trophy is a silver gilt cup and cover with two handles and a lid. It was made in 1877. The men's champion receives a replica of the trophy. The Ladies' Singles Trophy is a sterling silver plate known as the Venus Rosewater Dish. It is decorated with figures from **mythology**. The women's winner receives a small copy of the trophy. The winners of the Gentlemen's Doubles, Ladies' Doubles, and Mixed Doubles events each receive silver cups.

Wimbledon History

Wimbledon's history began when The All England Croquet Club was started in 1868. Soon after the club was formed, a new game was added to the list of club activities. The sport was originally known as Sphairistike. This is a Greek word that means "ball sports." Members of the club learned the new game. It was renamed lawn tennis. The game became one of the most popular sports at the club.

In 1877, the club changed its name to The All England Croquet and Lawn Tennis Club. Plans were made to hold the first tennis championship. The event was held in Wimbledon, off Worple Road. Twenty-two players competed in front of 200 spectators.

Tony Wilding won four straight Wimbledon singles titles from 1910 to 1913.

In the early years of Wimbledon, male tennis players wore long pants and long shirts. Sometimes, they wore sweaters. All players used wooden racquets.

Gentlemen's Singles was the only event, and Spencer Gore became the first champion. The Championships was a men's-only event until 1884. Ladies' Singles was introduced that year. Maud Watson won the first Ladies' Singles crown.

That same year, the first Gentlemen's Doubles event was introduced. William and Ernest Renshaw won the Gentlemen's Doubles. Ladies' Doubles and Mixed Doubles began in 1913.

Jimmy Connors was the Gentlemen's Singles champion at Wimbledon in 1974 and 1982.

In December of 1967, the LTA voted to make all lawn tennis tournaments in England open events. This meant that both amateur and professional athletes could compete. Before 1967, only amateur players were invited to play at Wimbledon.

In 1968, Rod Laver and Billie-Jean King became the first professional players to win the Wimbledon championship. They were the first players to receive money for winning the championship.

Wimbledon Traditions

Tennis fans have enjoyed eating strawberries and cream at Wimbledon since the tournament began. Each order must have a minimum of 10 strawberries. It is served in a small container or basket called a *punnet*.

More than 61,000 pounds (28,000 kilograms) of strawberries and 1,800 gallons (7,000 liters) of dairy cream are served during the tournament.

Rules of the Game

The rules used at Wimbledon have changed little since the game was invented. Most of the major changes happened in the first decade. Overhand serving by hitting the ball above the shoulders instead of below the waist was allowed. The net was lowered, and the size of the serving box was reduced in size.

1 The Serve

A server has two chances to hit the ball into the receiver's court. If the serve is out, it is called a **fault**. If the server misses twice, it is called a double fault. The server loses a point. If the ball touches the net but lands in the receiver's court, a re-serve is allowed. If that serve does not land in the receiver's court, it is a fault.

2 Singles/Doubles

In singles, one player is on each side of the net. They take turns serving every game and change ends every other game. The game of doubles is played with two teams of two. The court is wider, but the service area where the ball must land is the same.

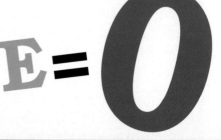

3 Terms of Scoring

It takes four points to win a game. A player must win by two points. In tennis, the first point is called 15, the second 30, and the third 40. If the game is tied at 40-40, the score is called **deuce**. The next point is called an ad, or advantage, point. The player who wins the ad point needs one more point to win the game. If that player loses the ad point, the score returns to deuce. The term love is used instead of zero. This means a player has no points or has not won a game.

LOVE = 0

4 Winning the Game

If a player misses the ball or hits it out of bounds, the opponent gets a point. Points win games, games win sets, and sets win matches. Four points win a game, six games win a set, and two or three sets win a match. A player must win a game by two points and a set by two games. Sometimes, a tiebreaker is used. If a set is tied 6–6, the first player to win the next seven points wins.

5 Sets

Gentlemen's matches are best-of-five sets. The first player to win three sets wins the match. Women play best-of-three matches. The first to win two sets wins the match. Mixed teams play best-of-three matches. The first team to win two sets wins the match.

Making the Call

Wimbledon officials are called **umpires**. There are many kinds of umpires. Chair umpires sit in a tall chair to the side of the net. They call out the score and can overrule all other officials. Line umpires stand behind the baseline. They decide whether a shot is in or out. The line umpires are assisted by a service line monitor called a **Cyclops**. It has one camera lens that looks like an eye. Professional tennis players hit the ball so fast that human eyes have trouble seeing it. The Cyclops helps the umpires determine whether a serve is in or out.

The Tennis Court

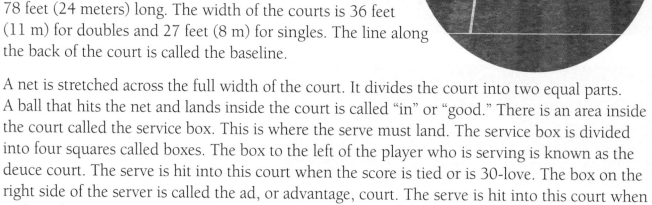

Tennis is played on a rectangular, flat surface called a court. The surface can be made of grass, clay, or hard materials, such as rubber or concrete. The courts used at Wimbledon are made of grass. They are 78 feet (24 meters) long. The width of the courts is 36 feet (11 m) for doubles and 27 feet (8 m) for singles. The line along the back of the court is called the baseline.

A net is stretched across the full width of the court. It divides the court into two equal parts. A ball that hits the net and lands inside the court is called "in" or "good." There is an area inside the court called the service box. This is where the serve must land. The service box is divided into four squares called boxes. The box to the left of the player who is serving is known as the deuce court. The serve is hit into this court when the score is tied or is 30-love. The box on the right side of the server is called the ad, or advantage, court. The serve is hit into this court when a player has a one-point lead in the game.

The game is played by trying to make the opposing player miss the ball or hit it out of bounds. The ball must be hit while it is in the air or on the first bounce. There are three types of tennis shots—the forehand, backhand, and volley. A forehand is hit to the side of the player's body with the front of the racquet. A backhand is hit across the player's body with the back of the racquet. A volley is hit when the player strikes the ball in the air before it bounces on the court.

Ball Boys and Ball Girls

Ball boys and ball girls retrieve balls that are hit out of bounds or off the playing surface. They kneel on the edge of the court or stand in the back of the court. Ball boys have been retrieving balls at Wimbledon since the 1920s. Ball girls first appeared in 1977. More than 300 young people apply to be ball boys and girls each year. About 200 are chosen to work the event. Ball boys and ball girls prepare for five months before the tournament. They must pass a written test about the rules of tennis.

THE TENNIS COURT

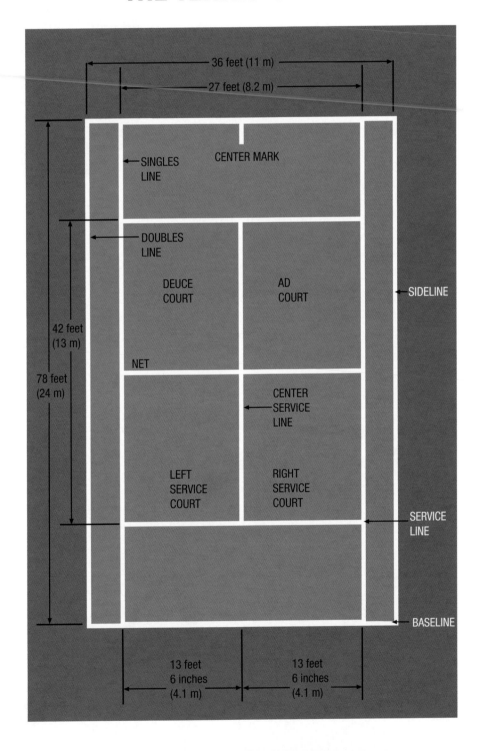

Tennis Equipment

A racquet, a tennis ball, and athletic shoes are the only equipment a person needs to play tennis. Professional players use special equipment, such as custom-made racquets. They will often bring at least four racquets to a match. This is in case a racquet breaks during a game. Racquets have four parts—the frame, the head, the strings, and the grip. Racquet frames are made from lightweight metals, such as graphite, boron, fiberglass, and magnesium. A racquet cannot be more than 29 inches (74 centimeters) long. The frame cannot be wider than 12.5 inches (32 cm).

A racquet's head is the section with strings. It cannot be longer than 15.5 inches (39 cm) or wider than 11.5 inches (29 cm). Strings can be made of many materials, such as nylon, gut, or titanium. Professional players prefer to use gut strings. Gut strings are made from dried animal intestines. They have more give, or flexibility, than other strings. Players can control their shots better using these types of strings. The grip is usually made of leather. This lets the player hold the racquet firmly. There are rules as to how big the grip can be.

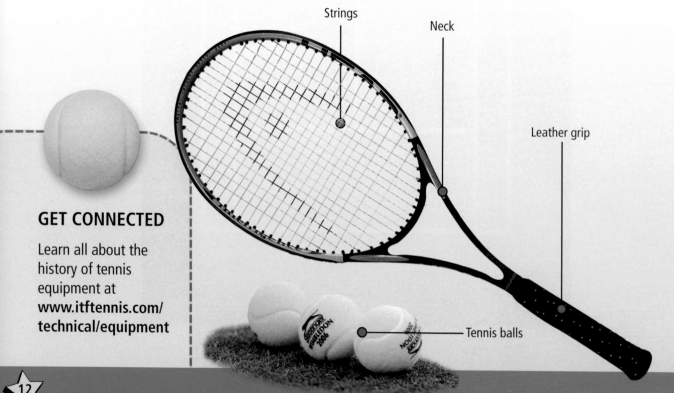

Strings

Neck

Leather grip

Tennis balls

GET CONNECTED

Learn all about the history of tennis equipment at **www.itftennis.com/ technical/equipment**

White shirt

White shorts

Racquet

Socks

Shoes

Today, the tennis balls used at Wimbledon are yellow. This makes it easier for umpires to tell when a shot is in or out. The ball has a rubber core filled with tightly-packed, or pressurized, air. This makes the ball bounce evenly and fairly.

There are shoes that are made just for tennis. They have special grips on the soles to stop players from sliding on the court.

Wimbledon's Dress Code

Wimbledon is the only tournament where players must wear white, or almost entirely white, clothing. Some players do not agree with this policy. Andre Agassi did not play at Wimbledon for many years because he wanted to wear the same kind of clothing he wore at other tournaments.

Wimbledon's strict dress code includes practice sessions. In 2002, Anna Kournikova wore black shorts under her tennis dress. Officials told her the shorts broke the dress code. She had to borrow a pair of men's white shorts.

Qualifying to Play

Players from around the world come to compete at Wimbledon. In 2006, the winners and runners-up of the five main events came from Switzerland, Spain, France, Belgium, the United States, Serbia, China, Argentina, Israel, and Russia.

To compete in the tournament, a player must submit an entry form six weeks before Wimbledon begins. A Committee of Management decides if the player will be accepted, rejected, or asked to play in the qualifying competition. The committee bases its decisions on the player's ranking in the Women's Tennis Association (WTA) and Association of Tennis Professionals (ATP) tours. If a player's ranking is high, he or she is usually allowed to enter the tournament without playing in a qualifying competition.

Some players with a low ranking are given wild card berths. This means they can enter the tournament without having to qualify. These are usually players who have done well in the past or are fan favorites. In 2001, Goran Ivanisevic became the first wild card player to win the Gentleman's Singles title.

The Order of Play board at Wimbledon tells fans who is playing and which players have advanced in the competition.

Under the International Tennis Federation's (ITF) rules, a player must be in good standing to compete at Wimbledon. This means that the player must not have been suspended by his or her national tennis association. This rule is rarely used. In 1973, Yugoslavia player Nikki Pilic was not allowed to compete. He had been suspended by his national association for refusing to play for his country in a international tournament. If the committee decides a player cannot enter the tournament directly, he or she must play in the qualifying competition.

The grass courts of Wimbledon will host the tennis events during the 2010 Summer Olympic Games.

In total, 128 men and women compete in each of the Gentlemen's and Ladies' Singles events. Sixty-four teams compete in the Gentlemen's and Ladies' Doubles events, and 48 teams compete in the Mixed Doubles event.

Players who lose a match are out of the tournament. This is called a single-elimination system. Each event has a winner and a runner-up. Both the winner and the runner-up receive a trophy. Every player that takes part in one of the five major events at the tournament receives a cash prize.

Qualifying Competition

The Qualifying competition is held at Roehampton, a district in London, England, the week before Wimbledon begins. The competition has three rounds. Players who win in all three rounds move on to Wimbledon. In Gentlemen's Singles, 16 players qualify. In Ladies' Singles, 12 players qualify. For Men's and Ladies' Doubles, four pairs qualify for each event. In 1977, American John McEnroe (right) became the first qualifier to advance all the way to the semifinals in the Gentlemen's Singles event.

Where They Play

Until 1922, Wimbledon was held at a location near Worple Road. The AELTC first rented the grounds in 1869 for croquet tournaments. In 1875, the first lawn tennis courts were made. A special locker room was built just for the club's tennis players.

The first courts built at Worple Road had a different shape than the courts that are used today. They were shaped like an hourglass. The courts were wide at the ends and narrow in the middle. Wimbledon's grounds changed over the years. Seating at the Worple Road location was expanded from 2,000 to 3,200.

Still, by 1920, the club had outgrown its home. New grounds and new facilities were needed. A man named Stanley Peach designed the new club.

In 1922, the new Wimbledon at Church Road was ready. It had 15 new grass courts and enough room to seat more than 14,000 spectators.

The last Wimbledon tournament held at the old grounds on Worple Road was played in 1921.

Wimbledon is the only Grand Slam tournament that is played on grass.

Wimbledon has continued to expand. Four new grass courts were built in 1980. A new No. 1, or main court, was added in 1997. There are plans to build a retractable or movable roof over the main court.

The new No. 1 court at Wimbledon seats more than 14,000 fans and features restaurants, bars, shops, and boutiques.

MEN'S AND LADIES' SINGLES CHAMPIONSHIPS 1997–2006

YEAR	MEN'S SINGLES	YEAR	LADIES' SINGLES
1997	P. Sampras	1997	M. Hingis
1998	P. Sampras	1998	J. Novotna
1999	P. Sampras	1999	L. Davenport
2000	P. Sampras	2000	V. Williams
2001	G. Ivanisevic	2001	V. Williams
2002	L.G. Hewitt	2002	S. Williams
2003	R. Federer	2003	S. Williams
2004	R. Federer	2004	M. Sharapova
2005	R. Federer	2005	V. Williams
2006	R. Federer	2006	A. Mauresmo

MEN'S AND LADIES' DOUBLES CHAMPIONSHIPS 1997–2006

YEAR	MEN'S DOUBLES	YEAR	LADIES' DOUBLES
1997	T. Woodbridge and M. Woodforde	1997	B. Fernandez and N. Zvereva
1998	J.F. Eltingh and P. Haarhuis	1998	M. Hingis and J. Novotna
1999	M.S. Bhupathi and L. Paes	1999	L. Davenport and C. Morariu
2000	T. Woodbridge and M. Woodforde	2000	V. Williams and S. Williams
2001	D. Johnson and J. Palmer	2001	L. Raymond and R. Stubbs
2002	J. Bjorkman and T. Woodbridge	2002	V. Williams and S. Williams
2003	J. Bjorkman and T. Woodbridge	2003	K. Clijsters and A. Sugiyama
2004	J. Bjorkman and T. Woodbridge	2004	C. Black and R. Stubbs
2005	S. Huss and W. Moodie	2005	C. Black and L. Huber
2006	B. Bryan and M. Bryan	2006	Z. Yan and J. Zheng

MIXED DOUBLES CHAMPIONSHIPS 1997–2006

YEAR	MIXED DOUBLES	YEAR	MIXED DOUBLES
1997	C. Suk and H. Sukova	2002	M. S. Bhupathi and E. Likhovteva
1998	M. Mirnyi and S. Williams	2003	L. Paes and M. Navratilova
1999	L. Paes and L. Raymond	2004	W. Black and C. Black
2000	D. Johnson and K. Y. Po	2005	M. S. Bhupathi and M. Pierce
2001	L. Friedl and D. Hantuchova	2006	A. Ram and V. Zvonareva

Mapping Wimbledon

NORTH
AMERICA

Pete Sampras

NORTH AMERICA

PACIFIC
OCEAN

ATLANTIC
OCEAN

Maria Bueno

SOUTH AMERICA

SOUTH
AMERICA

SOUTHERN
OCEAN

Wimbledon winners come
from around the world. There
have been winners from
Australia to Asia and Africa
to South America.

WIMBLEDON SINGLES WINNERS BY CONTINENT

- AFRICA – 1
- ASIA – 1
- AUSTRALIA – 59
- EUROPE – 110
- NORTH AMERICA – 109
- SOUTH AMERICA – 3

Scale

621 Miles
0   1,000 Kilometers

Roger Federer
EUROPE
EUROPE

Maria Sharapova
ASIA
ASIA

PACIFIC OCEAN

Jaroslav Drobny
AFRICA
AFRICA   INDIAN OCEAN

Leyton Hewitt
AUSTRALIA
AUSTRALIA

Women and Wimbledon

Wimbledon features the best female players from around the world. There have been as many legendary female players as men at Wimbledon. They include Steffi Graf, Martina Navratilova, and Suzanne Lenglen.

In the late 1800s and early 1900s, women played in long dresses with full-length sleeves. They often played wearing ankle-high boots. Women wore corsets, tight-fitting braces that covered the body from the chest to the hips. Women started the tradition of wearing white clothing at Wimbledon. They did it to hide the fact they were sweating heavily.

In 1919, Suzanne Lenglen was the first woman to wear lightweight clothing. She even refused to wear a corset. This allowed her to move more freely. Soon, all women players were wearing clothing that allowed them to move quickly.

GET CONNECTED

Find the latest news, results, rankings, and biographies of women players at **www.sony ericssonwtatour.com**.

Chris Evert was one of the first Wimbledon champions to place two hands on the racquet when hitting a backhand shot.

Lenglen challenged the clothing standards that were common at the time. She set an example for future female tennis players. Lenglen won her match against Dorothea Chambers, the defending Ladies' Singles champion. It was the first of five titles she would win in a row.

Some old rules have stayed in place at Wimbledon. If a female player is single, she is still referred to as "Miss." If the player is married, she is called by her married name.

In 1981, Mrs. John (Chris Evert) Lloyd defeated Miss Hanna Mandlikova. Mrs. Lloyd was the last married woman to win the singles title.

Lili de Alvarez of Spain played in three straight Wimbledon Ladies' Singles finals.

The tournament continues to divide its events into Gentlemen's and Ladies. Other tournaments use the terms "men" and "women" to describe the events.

The Size of the Prize

Until 2007, men made more money than women at Wimbledon. The 2006's Gentlemen's Singles champion, Roger Federer, received $1.28 million. The Ladies' Singles champion Amélie Mauresmo made $1.25 million. Women who played Women's Doubles and Mixed Doubles also received less money. The other Grand Slam tournaments paid women the same as men. Many players did not think this was fair. Men and women played the same number of sets in mixed doubles. Wimbledon officials agreed. In 2007, women began making the same money as men.

Historical Highlights

Over the years, Wimbledon has had its share of historical highlights. One of the early highlights was the success of Ernest and William Renshaw, a pair of British twins who won 13 titles between 1881 and 1889. Their victory streak was known as the "Renshaw Rush." That is because fans "rushed" to see them play. The Renshaw's were not the only brothers to have success at Wimbledon. In 1897, Laurie and Reggie Doherty started a successful streak that lasted 10 years.

During **World War I,** Wimbledon was not held for four years. During **World War II**, fire and ambulance services used the grounds. Soldiers stationed there used the grounds for drills. In October 1940, five 500-pound (227-kg) bombs hit center court, destroying more than 1,200 seats.

In 1973, 81 players from the ATP refused to attend Wimbledon. They were angry over the suspension of Yugoslavia player Nikki Pilic. It was the only strike in Wimbledon history.

In 1977, Wimbledon celebrated its 100th anniversary. More than 40 former singles champions were given commemorative medals. Queen Elizabeth II attended the tournament and presented Virginia Wade with the Ladies' Singles trophy. This was the last time a player from England won a Wimbledon Singles title. It also marked the last time that the Queen attended the tournament.

In 1984, Wimbledon celebrated the 100th anniversary of the Ladies' Singles Championships. American Martina Navratilova won the title.

Virginia Wade won three Grand Slam titles during her career, including the 1977 Wimbledon championship.

In 2003, Martina Navratilova became the oldest Grand Slam champion. She was 46 years and 261 days old when she won the Mixed Doubles title with Leander Paes.

Bjorn Borg usually wore a green pinstriped tennis shirt when he played at Wimbledon. He felt it brought him good luck.

WIMBLEDON RECORDS

WINNERS OF THE MOST GENTLEMEN'S SINGLES CHAMPIONSHIPS

7	Pete Sampras	1993–1995, 1997–2000
7	William Renshaw	1881–1886, 1889

WINNERS OF THE MOST GENTLEMEN'S DOUBLES CHAMPIONSHIPS

9	Todd Woodbridge	1993–1997, 2000, 2002–2004
8	Hugh "Laurie" Doherty	1897–1901, 1903–1905
8	Reggie Doherty	1897–1901, 1903–1905

WINNERS OF THE MOST LADIES' SINGLES CHAMPIONSHIPS

9	Martina Navratilova	1978, 1979, 1982–1987, 1990
8	Helen Wills Moody	1927–1930, 1932, 1933, 1935, 1938

WINNER OF THE MOST LADIES' DOUBLES CHAMPIONSHIPS

12	Elizabeth Ryan	1914, 1919–1923, 1925–1927, 1930, 1933, 1934

WINNERS OF THE MOST MIXED DOUBLES CHAMPIONSHIPS – GENTLEMEN

4	Owen Davidson	1967, 1971, 1973, 1974
4	Ken Fletcher	1963, 1965, 1966, 1968
4	Elias Seixas	1953–1956

WINNER OF THE MOST MIXED DOUBLES CHAMPIONSHIPS – LADIES

7	Elizabeth Ryan	1919, 1921, 1923, 1927, 1928, 1930, 1932

LEGENDS
and Current Stars

Bjorn Borg

Roger Federer

Gentleman's Singles Champion, 2003–2006

Roger Federer was born in Switzerland in 1981. He is known as a "five-tool" tennis player. This means his game is strong in five different ways. Federer has a fast and accurate serve. He can volley by playing close to the net and rally by hitting shots from the baseline. Federer can hit winning shots with both his forehand and backhand. In July of 2006, he won his fourth Wimbledon title in a row. Federer has won the French Open and the Australian Open three times. He is the only tennis player in history to win three different Grand Slam titles three times each.

Bjorn Borg

Gentlemen's Singles Champion, 1976–1980

Bjorn Borg was born in Sweden in 1956. He is the first non-British player to win five Wimbledon Gentlemen's Singles championships in a row. Borg's 1980 championship match against American John McEnroe lasted for nearly four hours. It was the second-longest final in Wimbledon history.

In his career, he won six French Open titles. Borg won both the French Open and Wimbledon three years in a row. No other player has been able to do that. Borg reached the finals of the United States Open four times, and he won 11 Grand Slam tournaments in 8 years. Borg retired from professional tennis in 1983. He was 26 years old.

Roger Federer

Serena Williams

Ladies Singles Champion, 2002, 2003

Ladies Doubles Champion, 2000, 2002

Serena Williams was born in the United States in 1981. She is known for her powerful game of tennis because she hits the ball very hard. Williams can serve the ball more than 100 miles (161 kilometers) per hour. She has won five titles at Wimbledon, including the Ladies' Singles championship in 2002 and 2003. Williams is one of only three African American women to win the Ladies' Singles title. In 2003, she won what was known as the "Serena Slam." She was the champion in all four Grand Slam tournaments at once. Williams won the 2002 French Open, U.S. Open, Wimbledon, and the 2003 Australian Open. She won the Australian Open again in 2005 and 2007.

Martina Navratilova

Martina Navratilova

Ladies' Singles Champion, 1978, 1979, 1982–1987, 1990

Ladies' Doubles Champion, 1976, 1979, 1981–1984, 1986

Martina Navratilova was born in what is now known as the Czech Republic in 1956. She became an American citizen in 1981. She was best known for her fitness and endurance. Navratilova played at Wimbledon for more than 30 years and won a record nine Ladies' Singles titles. In her career, Navratilova won 58 Grand Slam titles. She won 20 titles at Wimbledon, tying the record held by Billie-Jean King. Navratilova won every Grand Slam tournament at least twice during her 32 years as a professional tennis player.

Serena Williams

Famous Firsts

William Renshaw was the first player to win six consecutive Gentlemen's Singles championships at Wimbledon. He defeated his brother Ernest to win three of those titles.

The first 21 Ladies' Singles titles at Wimbledon were won by women from Great Britain. In 1905, American May Sutton became the first person from North America to win the championship. Australian Norman Brookes was the first Gentlemen's Singles champion who was not born in Great Britain. He captured the title in 1907. In 1919, all five major Wimbledon titles were won by foreign-born players for the first time.

Althea Gibson played professional golf when her tennis career ended.

Cara Black and playing partner Liezel Huber (right) have won two Grand Slam women's doubles titles.

Althea Gibson was the first African American Wimbledon champion. She won the Ladies' Singles title in 1957. It was only her second appearance at the tournament.

In 1961, Christine Truman and Angela Mortimer faced each other in the Ladies' Singles final. This was the first time that two British women had competed in the championship match since 1914. Mortimer won the title in three sets.

In 1985, Boris Becker became the first unseeded player to win the Gentleman's Singles title. He was not one of the world's top 16 players when he entered the tournament. In addition to being the lowest-ranked player to win, Becker was the youngest Wimbledon champion. He was just 17 years old when he won the event.

Boris Becker won the Gentleman's Singles title at Wimbledon in 1985, 1986, and 1989.

Liezel Huber won the Ladies' Doubles crown in 2005. She was the first player born in South Africa to win a major event at Wimbledon.

Winning at Wimbledon

The ceremony that follows the completion of the Ladies' and Gentlemen's Singles finals at Wimbledon is a grand tradition of the tournament. Tournament officials, umpires, ball boys, and ball girls all gather at center court. The men and women's winners are presented with their championship trophies by the Duke and Duchess of Kent, who are members of the British Royal Family. The winners parade around the court, displaying their trophies for the fans and the television audience.

The Rise of Wimbledon

1875

The All England Croquet Club starts playing lawn tennis. Locker rooms for the players are built, and money is given to buy equipment.

1877

Spencer Gore becomes the first Wimbledon champion. He defeats William Marshall in three sets.

1884

The first Ladies' Singles event is played. Gentlemen's Doubles is also introduced.

1897

Reggie and Laurie Doherty win the first of five straight Gentlemen's Doubles titles at Wimbledon.

1905

American May Sutton wins the Ladies' Singles event at Wimbledon.

1907

Australian Norman Brookes becomes the first male champion from outside Great Britain to win the Gentlemen's Singles event.

1913

Ladies' Doubles and Mixed Doubles are played for the first time at Wimbledon. Winifred McNair and Dora Boothby win the Ladies' Doubles event, while Hope Crisp and Agnes Tuckey win the first Mixed Doubles title.

1915–1918

Wimbledon is temporarily halted during **World War I**.

1922

Wimbledon moves to Church Road from its old home near Worple Road. The new home has improved facilities.

1968

Billie-Jean King and Rod Laver become the first singles winners at Wimbledon to receive prize money.

1970

Australia's Margaret Court wins her third and final Ladies' Singles title by defeating Billie-Jean King 14–12 and 11–9.

1977

Wimbledon celebrates 100 years of competition. The event is called The Centenary Championships.

1997

A new No. 1 Court, a new broadcast center, and two extra grass courts are built at Wimbledon.

QUICK FACTS

- Wimbledon starts six weeks before the first Monday in August.

- The last time a wooden racquet was used at Wimbledon was in 1987.

- Martina Hingis was the youngest player to win a major title at Wimbledon. She was 15 years and 282 days old when she won the Ladies' Doubles title in 1992.

- Wimbledon has its own on-site museum called The Wimbledon Lawn Tennis Museum.

Test Your Knowledge

1 How long does Wimbledon last?

2 When was the first Wimbledon held?

3 Who was the first Wimbledon champion?

7 When was the last wooden racquet used at Wimbledon?

8 Who was the first non-British player to win five singles titles in a row?

9 Who was the first African American Wimbledon champion?

10 How many Wimbledon titles did Martina Navratilova win?

4 Who can compete in an open tennis tournament?

5 What are the four Grand Slam tennis tournaments?

6 When did Wimbledon move to its present location?

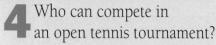

ANSWERS: 1) two weeks **2)** 1877 **3)** Spencer Gore **4)** amateurs and professionals **5)** the French Open, the Australian Open, the U.S. Open, and Wimbledon **6)** 1922 **7)** 1987 **8)** Bjorn Borg **9)** Althea Gibson **10)** 20

Further Research

Many books and websites provide information on the Wimbledon. To learn more about the tournament, borrow books from the library, or surf the Internet.

Books to Read

Most libraries have computers that connect to a database for researching information. If you input a key word, you will be provided with a list of books in the library that contain information on that topic. Non-fiction books are arranged numerically, using their call number. Fiction books are organized alphabetically by the author's last name.

Online Sites

Wimbledon's website, **www.wimbledon.org**, contains information about the history, rules, background, and events related to tennis for men and women.

BBC Sport Tennis has a great deal of information about the game. Go to **http://news.bbc.co.uk/sport**, and click on "Tennis."

The United States Tennis Association website, **www.usta.com**, has scores, player profiles, rankings, and tournament information.

Glossary

All England Lawn Tennis Club (AELTC): the private club that organizes The Championships, Wimbledon

Cyclops: nickname for the electronic monitors used to watch the court's service lines

deuce: when both players have reached 40 points

doubles: a tennis game played between two teams of two players who are on opposite sides of the net

fault: when the server hits the ball out of bounds, misses it entirely, or steps on the baseline while serving

Grand Slam: winning all four major tennis tournaments in the same year

lawn tennis: a racquet game played on grass

mythology: a set of stories or beliefs

singles: tennis game played between two players who are on opposite sides of the net

tournament: series of games or contests between players who compete for a common prize or award

umpires: officials who keep the score, judge if the ball is in bounds, and interpret rules

World War I: war that lasted from 1914 to 1918 and included the continents of Asia, Australia, Europe, and North America

World War II: war that lasted from 1939 to 1945 and included the continents of Asia, Africa, Australia, Europe, North America, and South America

Index